LAMDA
SOLO SPEECHES FOR MEN
(1800–1914)

LAMDA
SOLO SPEECHES FOR MEN
(1800–1914)

Edited by SHAUN McKENNA

PUBLISHED BY
OBERON BOOKS
FOR THE LONDON ACADEMY OF
MUSIC AND DRAMATIC ART

First published in 1997 for LAMDA Ltd.
by Oberon Books Ltd.
(incorporating Absolute Classics)
521 Caledonian Road, London N7 9RH
Tel: 0171 607 3637 / Fax: 0171 607 3629
e-mail: oberon.books@btinternet.com
www.oberonbooks.com

Reprinted with corrections in 2004.

A catalogue record for this book is available from the British Library.

ISBN 1 84002 421 6

Cover design: Society
Cover photograph: John Haynes

Printed in Great Britain by Antony Rowe Ltd, Chippenham.

Contents

Introduction

Solo Speeches for Men (1800–1914) contains a selection of monologues from the lesser-known plays of the nineteenth century, appropriate for both the actor and examination candidate. The collection includes extracts for a range of ages, increasing in emotional complexity and technical challenge as they progress.

Until the latter part of the century, when the great revolutionary playwrights – Ibsen, Strindberg, Chekhov, Wilde and Shaw – came to the fore, nineteenth-century theatre was dominated more by star performers than by remarkable playwrights. This is particularly true of the English repertoire. As a result, this collection contains a substantial number of speeches from European plays. Where such names as Chekhov, Ibsen and Wilde appear, I have selected speeches from minor or little-known plays, rather than the universally popular ones.

Dates, brief biographical details of the authors and an indication of the context of the speech have been given in every case. The European speeches have been specially translated for this collection by Simon Parker, Mary Patrick and Veronica George.

It is interesting to note how many of the speeches from English plays deal with the outraging of conventional morality, particularly with regard to women. Many of the serious plays of the later nineteenth century dealt with 'issues' and sometimes the importance of the subject matter led playwrights to skimp on developing fully-rounded characters. The speeches in this collection have been selected to minimise this.

A companion volume of *Solo Speeches for Women (1800–1914)* is also published by LAMDA and Oberon Books.

Shaun McKenna

JUSTICE (1910)

by John Galsworthy

John Galsworthy (1867–1933) was a prolific writer, best-remembered for his series of nine novels about the Forsyte family. He was called to the Bar in 1890 but never practised. He was a prolific and successful playwright whose plays include, apart from those represented in this volume, *The Fugitive* (1913), *The Skin Game* (1920), *Loyalties* (1922), *Old English* (1924) and *Escape* (1926).

> *WILLIAM FALDER is a pale, good-looking young man of twenty-three with quick, scared eyes. He is appearing in court charged with altering a cheque, a result of his liaison with a married woman.*

FALDER: I was having my breakfast when she came. Her dress was all torn and she was gasping and couldn't seem to get her breath at all; there were the marks of fingers round her throat; her arm was bruised, and the blood had got into her eyes dreadfully. It frightened me, and then when she told me, I felt – I felt – well – it was too much for me. (*Hardening suddenly.*) If you'd seen it, having the feelings for her that I had, you'd have felt the same, I know. When she left me – because I had to go to the office – I was out of my senses for fear that he'd do it again, and thinking what I could do. I couldn't work – all the morning I was like that – simply couldn't fix my mind on anything. I couldn't think at all. I seemed to have to keep moving. When Davis – the other clerk – gave me the cheque – he said, 'It'll do you good, Will, to have a run with this. You seem half off your chump this morning.' Then when I had it in my hand – I don't know how it came, but it just flashed across me that if

I just put the *ty* and the nought there would be the money to get her away. It just came and went – I never thought of it again. Then Davis went out to his luncheon, and I don't really remember what I did till I'd pushed the cheque through to the cashier under the rail. I remember his saying, 'Notes?' Then I suppose I knew what I'd done. Anyway, when I got outside I wanted to chuck myself under a bus; but it seemed I was in for it, so I thought at any rate I'd save her. Of course the tickets I got for the passage and the little I gave her's been wasted, and all, except what I was obliged to spend on myself, I've restored. I keep thinking over and over however it was I came to do it, and how I can't have it all again to do differently.

Available in *Late Victorian Plays*, Ed: George Rowell, The World's Classics and *The Plays of John Galsworthy*, Duckworth.

HINDLE WAKES (1912)
by Stanley Houghton

Cheshire-born Stanley Houghton (1881–1913) worked in his father's cotton business until becoming involved with the growing repertory theatre movement of the early 1900s. His plays include *The Reckoning* (1906), *Fancy Free* (1911) and *The Fifth Commandment* (1913). *Hindle Wakes* dealt with controversial material for its time and is set in the Lancashire village of Hindle.

> *ALAN JEFFCOTE, a mill-owner's son, has spent a weekend away with FANNY HAWTHORN, a girl in her twenties. Now scandal looms and the families are trying to patch up a marriage that nobody really wants but which would suit social convention. The piece requires a Lancashire accent. ALAN is taking to BEATRICE, the girl he is sweet on.*

ALAN: I'm not a proper cad, Bee. I haven't been telling her one story and you another. It was all an accident, like. It wasn't all arranged. I shouldn't like you to think that, Bee. I ran across her at Blackpool. I went there in the car with George Ramsbottom. He's a pal. He made himself scarce. I dare say he picked something up himself.

Of course I knew her before Blackpool. There's not so many pretty girls in Hindle that you can miss one like Fanny Hawthorn. I knew her well enough, but on the straight, mind you. I'd hardly spoken to her before I ran into her at the Tower in Blackpool. We'd just had dinner at the Metropole Grill-room, George and I, and I daresay had drunk about as much champagne as was good for us. We looked in at the Tower for a lark, and we ran into Fanny in the Ballroom. She had a girl with her – Mary – Mary something or other. I forget. Anyhow, George took Mary on and I went with Fanny. Next day I got her to come with me in the car. We went to Llandudno. There's not much more to say. What else do you want me to tell you?

Yes, Bee, I suppose I did think about you. But you weren't there, you see, and she was. That was what did it. Being near her and looking at her lips. Then I forgot everything else. Oh, I know. I'm a beast. I couldn't help it. I suppose you can never understand. It's too much for you to see the difference. Fanny was just an amusement – a lark. I thought of her as a girl to have a bit of fun with. Going off with her was like going off and getting tight for once in a way. You wouldn't care for me to do that, but if I did you wouldn't think very seriously about it. You wouldn't want to break off our engagement for that. If wonder if you can look on this affair of Fanny's as something like getting tight – only worse. I'm ashamed of myself, just as I should be if you caught me drunk. I can't defend myself.

Available in *Late Victorian Plays*, Ed: George Rowell, The World's Classics.

THE MOB (1914)

by John Galsworthy

See note on Galsworthy on page 9.

ALAN STEEL is 'a thin-faced young man with the eyes of one who can attach himself to people and suffer with them.' He works for MP STEPHEN MORE, who has just made a highly controversial speech in the House of Commons. Here, he tells MORE's wife what has just happened.

STEEL: We were here – he slipped away from me somehow. He must have gone straight down to the House. I ran over, but when I got in under the Gallery he was speaking already. They expected something – I never heard it so still there. He gripped them from the first word – deadly – every syllable. He got some of those fellows. But all the time, under the silence, you could feel a – a sort of – of – current going round. And then Sherratt – I think it was – began it, and you saw the anger rising in them; but he kept them down – his quietness! The feeling! I've never seen anything like it there. Then there was a whisper all over the House that fighting had begun. And the whole thing broke out – a regular riot – as if they could have killed him. Someone tried to drag him down by the coat-tails, but he shook him off, and went on. Then he stopped dead and walked out, and the noise dropped like a stone. The whole thing didn't last five minutes. It *was* fine, Mrs More; like – like lava; he was the only cool person there. I wouldn't have missed it for anything – it was grand!

Available in *The Plays of John Galsworthy*, Duckworth.

THE VOYSEY INHERITANCE (1905)
by Harley Granville-Barker

Harley Granville-Barker (1877–1946) was an actor, dramatist and critic whose *Prefaces to Shakespeare* are still essential reading. His plays include *The Marrying of Ann Leete* (1899), *Waste* (1906), *The Madras House* (1910) and *His Majesty* (1928).

> *EDWARD VOYSEY has 'a refined face, but self-consciousness takes the place in it of imagination and in suppressing traits of brutality in his character, it looks as though the young man has suppressed his sense of humour, too.' He has just discovered that his father's successful business is based on shady dealing. Here, EDWARD confronts VOYSEY SNR.*

EDWARD: I should like you now, sir, if you don't mind, to drop with me all these protestations about putting the firm's affairs straight, and all your anxieties and sacrifices to that end. I see now, of course, what a cleverer man than I could have seen yesterday…that for some time, ever since, I suppose, you recovered from the first shock and got used to the ble dealing, this hasn't been your object at all. You used your clients' capital to produce your own income…to bring us up and endow us with. Booth's ten thousand pounds, what you are giving Ethel on her marriage… It's odd it never struck me yesterday that my own pocket money as a boy was probably withdrawn from some client's account. You've been very generous to us all, Father. I suppose about half the sum you've spent on us would have put things right, at some time or other. You allow my sister three hundred a year

– and yet you've never attempted to put a single account straight. Since it isn't lunacy, sir, I can only conclude that you enjoy being in this position. If I'm to remain with the firm it had better be with a very clear understanding of how things are. I will stay with the firm, but I want to make one condition. And I want some information. Have you ever under stress of circumstances done worse than just make use of a client's capital? You boasted to me yesterday that no one had ever suffered in pocket because of you. Is that absolutely true?

Thank you, sir. The condition I wish to make is that we should really do what we have pretended to be doing – try and put the accounts straight. One by one. I shall begin, Father, by halving the salary I draw from the firm. And I think you cannot give Ethel the five thousand pounds dowry. The money isn't yours to give.

Available in *Granville-Barker: Plays One*, Methuen.

THE NIGHT BEFORE THE TRIAL (1890s)
by Anton Chekhov
translated by Simon Parker

Anton Chekhov (1860–1904) is one of the founding fathers of modern drama, and his work with Konstantin Stanislavsky at the Moscow Arts Theatre was seminal. His naturalistic masterpieces include *The Seagull* (1896), *Uncle Vanya* (1897), *The Three Sisters* (1901) and *The Cherry Orchard* (1904). He also wrote a number of short one-act comedies, or vaudevilles, of which this is one.

> *ZAYTSEV, a traveller, has just arrived with his suitcase at a coaching inn. It is a cold winter night.*

ZAYTSEV: What a terrible smell! You can't breathe in here. There's a nasty sour smell all mixed up with sealing-wax and bed-bugs. Ugh! Call me at six in the morning, will you? And have my carriage ready then, I'm due in town by nine.

> *He starts to remove his coat and boots.*

It's absolutely freezing. I'm so cold, my brain has congealed. I feel as though I'd been covered with snow, sed in cold water and frozen to an icicle – and then beaten to within an inch of my life. What with this dreadful blizzard and these impossible snow-drifts, I'd have been done for out there in another five minutes. And for what? If I was going to meet a lady or collect a grand inheritance, I wouldn't mind so much. But no – I'm on the road to ruin. What a miserable prospect. I'm called to the assizes in town tomorrow and I'm charged with attempted bigamy, forging grandmama's will to the tune of just three hundred roubles, and the attempted murder of a billiards-maker. I'm bound to be sent down – the jury will see to that! Here today, gaol tomorrow. And probably Siberia in six months time. Brr! The only way out of this mess – at least that I can see – is to appeal to a dear old trusty friend. He won't let me down if the jury finds against me. Here he is.

Takes out a large pistol from his suitcase.

Good, loyal old chap. I swapped him with Cheprakov for a couple of hounds. (*To the pistol.*) Who's beautiful, then? Shooting myself with you will be a real pleasure. Are you loaded? (*Answering himself in a reedy voice.*) I certainly am. (*Own voice.*) I bet you'll go off with a splendid bang. (*Pistol's voice.*) One hell of a bang. (*Own voice.*) Yes, I just bet you will. Time for beddybyes.

He puts the pistol away.

The moment they bring in a guilty verdict, I'll pull out my friend, hold it to my head and put a bullet through my brains. Then that will be that! Brr! Isn't there a fire anywhere? Brr!

A different translation is available in *Chekhov: Short Plays*, Ed: Ronald Hingley, Oxford.

MONEY (1840)
by Edward Bulwer-Lytton

Edward Bulwer-Lytton (1803–73) wrote a number of successful plays including *The Duchess de la Vallière* (1837), *The Lady of Lyons* (1838) and *Richelieu* (1839). *Money* was written in close association with star actor William Macready, who played Alfred Evelyn. Bulwer-Lytton determined to make an important contribution to comedy involving 'stronger and more real grave passions than the comedy of the last century'.

> *ALFRED EVELYN was secretary to SIR JOHN VESEY and in love with his cousin, CLARA GLAS. CLARA refused his offer of marriage – EVELYN believes that this was because of his poverty. Unexpectedly, EVELYN benefits from a legacy of half a million pounds and finds himself fawned upon by men who previously despised him. Here, he talks to his solicitor, GRAVES, of the unfairness of life.*

EVELYN: Graves, of all my new friends – and their name is Legion – you are the only one I esteem; there is sympathy between us – we take the same views of life. I am cordially glad to see another man as miserable as myself. Sit down and listen, I want a confidant. Left fatherless when yet a boy, my mother grudged herself food to give me education. Someone told her that learning was better than house and land – that's a lie, Graves, a scandalous lie! On the strength of that I was put to school – sent to a college, a sizar. Do you know what a sizar is? In pride he is a gentleman – in knowledge he is a scholar – and he crawls about, amidst gentlemen and scholars, with the livery of a pauper on his back. I carried off the great prizes – I became distinguished – I looked to a high degree, leading to a fellowship; that is, an independence for myself, a home for my mother. One day, a young lord insulted me – I retorted – he struck me – refused apology – refused redress. I was a sizar, a pariah, a thing to be struck! Sir, I was at least a man and I horsewhipped him in the hall before the eyes of the whole College. A few days and the lord's chastisement was forgotten. The next day the sizar was expelled – the career of a life blasted! That is the difference between rich and poor; it takes a whirlwind to move the one – a breath may uproot the other. I came to London. As long as my mother lived, I had one to toil for; and I did toil – did hope – did struggle to be something yet. She died. Then, somehow, my spirit broke – I resigned myself to my fate; the Alps above me seemed too high to ascend – I ceased to care what became of me. At last I submitted to be the poor relation – the hanger-on and gentleman lackey of Sir John Vesey. But I had an object in that – there was one in that house whom I had loved at first sight. I fancied I was loved in return – and was deceived. Not an hour before I inherited this mighty wealth I confessed my love and was rejected because I was poor. Now I detest that girl. I've already, thank Heaven, taken some revenge on her. I've bribed Sharp to say that Mordaunt's letter to me contained a codicil leaving Clara glas twenty thousand pounds. I've paid the money – she's no longer a dependant. No one can insult her now. She owes it all to me and does not guess it, man. Owes it to me – me, whom she rejected, me the poor scholar. There's some spite in that, eh?

Available in *English Plays of the Nineteenth Century, Volume 3*, Ed: M R Booth, Oxford.

THE SILVER BOX (1906)
by John Galsworthy

See note on Galsworthy on page 9.

JONES is a violent young working-class man, here talking to his downtrodden wife.

JONES: I've had enough o' this tryin' for work. Why should I go round and round lookin' for work like a bloomin' squirrel in a cage. 'Give us a job, sir.' – 'Take a man on' – 'Got a wife and three children' – Sick of it, I am. I'd sooner lie here and rot. 'Jones, you come and join the demonstration; come and 'old a flag and listen to the ruddy orators, and go 'ome as empty as you came.' There's some that seems to like that – the sheep! When I go seekin' for a job now, and see the brutes lookin' me up and down, it's like a thousand serpents in me. I'm not askin' for any treat. A man wants to sweat hisself silly and ain't allowed – that's a rum start, ain't it? A man wants to sweat his soul out to keep the breath in him and ain't allowed – that's justice – that's freedom and all the rest of it.

You're so milky mild. You don't know what goes on inside o' me. I'm done with the silly game. If they want me, let 'em come for me.

I've tried and done with it, I tell you. I've never been afraid of what's before me. You mark my words – if you think they've broke my spirit, you're mistook. I'll lie and rot sooner than ask 'em again. What makes you stand like that – you long-suffering, Gawd-forsaken image – that's why I can't keep my hands off you. So now you know. Work! You can work, but you haven't the spirit of a louse.

Available in *The Plays of John Galsworthy*, Duckworth.

A WOMAN OF NO IMPORTANCE (1893)
by Oscar Wilde

Oscar Fingal O'Flahertie Wills Wilde (1854–1900) is one of the most famous figures in late nineteenth century drama, author of such plays as *Lady Windermere's Fan* and *Salomé* (both 1892), *An Ideal Husband* and *The Importance of Being Earnest* (both 1895).

> *Young GERALD ARBUTHNOT is making his way in the world and has been offered a position by LORD ILLINGWORTH. He does not know that ILLINGWORTH is his father. Here, GERALD tells his mother, who is horrified by the connection, of his plans for the future.*

GERALD: I am so happy tonight, mother. I have never been so happy. Of course I am sorry to leave you. You are the best mother in the whole world. But after all, as Lord Illingworth says, it is impossible to live in such a place as Wrockley. You don't mind it. But I'm ambitious; I want something more than that. I want to have a career. I want to do something that will make you proud of me, and Lord Illingworth is going to help me. He is going to do everything for me.

How changeable you are. You don't seem to know your own mind for a single moment. An hour and a half ago in the drawing-room you agreed to the whole thing: now you turn round and make objections, and try to make me give up my one chance in life. Yes, my one chance. You don't suppose that men like Lord Illingworth are to be found every day, do you, mother? It is very strange that when I have had such a wonderful piece of good luck, the one person to put difficulties in my way should be my own mother. Besides, you know, mother, I love Hester Worsley. Who could help loving her? I love her more than I have ever told you, far more. Don't you understand now, mother, what it means to be Lord Illingworth's secretary? To start life like that is to find a career ready for one – before one – waiting for one. If I were Lord Illingworth's secretary I could ask Hester to be my wife. As a wretched bank clerk with a hundred a year it would be an impertinence.

You have always tried to crush my ambition, haven't you? You have told me that the world is a wicked place, that success is not worth having, that society is shallow, and all that sort of thing. Well, I don't believe it, mother. I think the world must be delightful. I think society must be exquisite. I think success is a thing worth having. You have been wrong in all that you taught me, mother, quite wrong. Lord Illingworth is a successful man. He is a fashionable man. He is a man who lives in the world and for it. Well, I would give anything to be just like Lord Illingworth.

Available in *The Complete Works of Oscar Wilde*, Collins.

LEONCE AND LENA (1836)
by Georg Büchner
translated by Veronica George

Georg Büchner, who died at the age of only twenty-four, left behind three plays – *Danton's Death* (1835), *Leonce and Lena,* and the fragmentary *Woyzeck* (1837). None of the plays were performed during his lifetime. He was a biologist, a radical student and was pursued by the authorities for sedition.

> *This comedy is set in a fairy-tale kingdom. PRINCE LEONCE of Pi and PRINCESS LENA of Po are betrothed but each is so frightened of being married that they flee. In the countryside, they meet and fall in love – not knowing who the other is. Finally, they arrive back at the Court of Pi pretending to be life-sized puppets. VALERIO, LEONCE's companion, introduces them to the Court.*

VALERIO: Ladies and gentlemen, the two world-famous automata have arrived. I might even say that I'm the third and most remarkable of the pair, only I don't know who I am – which shouldn't really surprise anyone, by the way, as I've no idea what I'm talking about. Indeed, I've no idea whether I've got any idea – which makes it likely that someone else is doing the talking and I'm just a cunning arrangement of pipes and windbags.

Do you follow me so far? No? Never mind, neither do I.

My lords, ladies and gentlemen, I present two persons of different sexes, one male, one female, one little lady and one little gentleman. All a mechanical trick – nothing but papier-maché and watch-springs. Each has a superfine ruby-mounted spring under the little toenail of the right foot. Press it ever so gently and the mechanism will run for a good fifty years. They are so well-made that if you didn't know they were puppets, you'd think they were real human beings. You'd go to parties with them. You'd have lunch with them. You'd dance with them. You'd admire their personalities. They get up early, have clean habits, charming manners and good digestions – which means they have clear consciences. The lady can sing all the latest opera tunes and the gentleman changes his shirt every day. Look carefully – interesting things are happening to them! The mechanism of love has just started to operate. He has given her flowers a few times and she has blushed and looked away, modestly. And we all know what happens next, don't we? Marriage!

(*With a flourish.*) Ladies and gentlemen, I am proud to present...THE EFFIGIES!

A different translation is available in *The Plays of Georg Büchner*, Oxford.

MARY STUART (1800)

by Friedrich Schiller
translated by Veronica George

Friedrich Schiller (1759–1805) is the most famous Classical German playwright. He was born in Marbach, near Stuttgart and died in Weimar. His plays include *The Robbers* (1780), *Don Carlos* (1787), *Wallenstein* (1799), *The Maid of Orleans* (1801) and *William Tell* (1803). He is the leading example of the 'Sturm und Drang' (Storm and Stress) school of German Romanticism and was much concerned with notions of free will and individual liberty. This, his most famous play, tells the tragic story of Mary Queen of Scots and, like many of his other historical dramas, takes considerable liberties with history – including a meeting between Mary and Queen Elizabeth.

MARY, the Catholic Queen of Scots, is the centre of a number of plots to depose the Protestant English Queen, ELIZABETH I. As a result, she has been imprisoned. MORTIMER is the nephew of SIR AMYAS PAULET, MARY's gaoler at Fotheringhay Castle, and secretly a convert to Catholicism. Here he visits MARY to pledge his allegiance to her cause and to explain how his conversion came about through the CARDINAL DE GUISE, MARY's spiritual mentor.

MORTIMER

When my Lord Cardinal returned to France
I travelled on to Rheims, where Jesuits
Are piously and strictly training priests
Who will return to lead the English church.
There I met Scotland's noble Morgan, with
Your loyal Lesley and the learned Bishop

Of Ross, now exiled miserably in France.
My faith grew stronger as I spent my time
With men like these. Then, one day, in the house
Of my Lord Bishop, what should catch my eye
But the fair portrait of a wondrous beauty.
It caught my soul – I gazed into its depths –
It overwhelmed me – and the Bishop said,
'Well may you gaze in wonder, for you see
The loveliest woman living on this earth –
The saddest, too – a martyr for the faith –
And it is in your homeland that she suffers'.
The more he spoke, the more it broke my heart.
He eloquently told me your great grief
And of your enemies' fierce tyranny.
He showed me, too, the Tudor family tree,
Proved you alone should sit on England's throne,
Not she who does, usurping bastard child
Whose very father had rejected her.
I knew I must learn more: I spoke to scribes,
To lawyers, men who understood the ways
In which true genealogies are read.
They all confirmed your claim. And now I know
The only wrong you do to England's Queen
Is that you have more right than she to rule.
At the same time, I heard you were removed
From Talbot's keeping and, by a great chance,
Were placed here with my uncle as your keeper.
This was the hand of God, a miracle
Designed by Heaven so I could rescue you.
The happiness I feel in being here,
Able to breathe this prison air with you
Is boundless. And I understand at last
Why she is right to keep you hidden here.

For if the men of England could behold
Their rightful Queen, as I do now, so pent
Then every youth would straightaway rebel,
Then every sword would be drawn from its sheath
And bloody civil war would monstrously
Stride through the country.

Different translations are available in *Five German Tragedies*, Penguin, and in *Schiller: Five Plays*, Oberon Books.

MEDEA (1820)

by Franz Grillparzer
translated by Mary Patrick

Franz Grillparzer (1791–1872) was Viennese and wrote this version of the famous Greek tragedy when he was in his late 20s. He was much inspired by classical models and also wrote plays based on the legends of Hero and Leander and Sappho. *Medea* is the third play in a trilogy on the tale of Jason and the Argonauts.

MEDEA has helped to obtain for JASON the Golden Fleece from the KING OF IOLCUS, and they have returned to his homeland of Corinth. Here, a HERALD has arrived to tell how JASON and MEDEA obtained the Fleece by deception.

HERALD

The King fell ill with fever, and so strange
Were all his symptoms – perhaps already fatal –
His daughters called Medea to their aid
To heal him – for they knew her reputation
With medicines, with potions and with cures.
She went with them but said if the King lived
The fee she wanted was the Golden Fleece –
A doom, she called it – and the girls agreed.
She entered the King's bedroom and she spoke
Strange incantations, dark, mysterious words.
The King sank deeper, deeper into sleep.
Medea said his blood must then be purged
And deeply cut into the royal veins.
The daughters saw their father's fever fade

And felt great pleasure as they bound his wounds.
Medea left, she says. The daughters also.
The King was sleeping peacefully at last.
But then a sudden, piercing cry was heard,
The daughters rushed into their father's room
To a see a frantic, terrifying sight:
The poor old man lay writhing on the ground,
The bandages that bound his arms were burst,
And streams of blood were pouring from his
                                          wounds.
He struggled towards the altar where the Fleece
Had always hung. It was not there. That night,
Medea slung the Fleece around her shoulders
And strode away in triumph. She was seen!
Never again shall witchcraft and low guile
Infect our land. I have come here today
To declare Jason banished, for he knew
Medea's plan and he colluded in it.
His feet must never more touch Grecian soil!
His wife, his children – all must bear his sin!
Three days and nights we give him for provision
To leave this land. If any give him aid
The self-same punishment descends on them.

Pointing to the four points of the compass.

Banished, Jason and Medea.
Jason and Medea, banished!
Banished!
Jason and Medea.

A different translation is available in *Five German Tragedies*,
Penguin.

ANATOL (1892)
by Arthur Schnitzler
translated by Simon Parker

Arthur Schnitzler (1862–1931) was Viennese. Much of his work was controversial during his lifetime, including his most famous play, *La Ronde* (1903), a series of sexual encounters between ten characters eventually forming a closed chain of relationships. Schnitzler's work was heavily influenced by the work of Sigmund Freud. His other works include *The Adventure of His Life* (1891), *Liebelei* (1895), *The Veil of Beatrice* (1900) and *The Call of Life* (1906). *Anatol* is a play-cycle made up of seven short two- or three-handed pieces, all dealing with some aspect of male/female relationships. This extract is from *Episode*.

ANATOL is an unreformed young rake, who wishes to seduce all women in order to prove them unfaithful. Here he is talking to his friend, MAX.

ANATOL: Today I know I'm not one of the race of giants – isn't that sad? – Still, I'm used to the idea. But then… She was a creature who crossed my path and whom I… Yes, the more I think about it, the more I think that I did actually destroy her. It's really the most beautiful thing that I've ever experienced. I can't talk about it. It's a mundane story, banal. You wouldn't understand how beautiful it was. It was beautiful because it happened to me. I was sitting in front of the piano one evening – I lived in a small room in those days. We had known each other for two hours. My red and green lamp was burning – it plays a part in the story, that lamp. She was at my feet, her head in my lap, and the lamp cast green and red colours into her rather messed-up hair. I was playing the piano, just improvising – and only with my left hand. She held my right to her lips. That was all. There's nothing else to it. I'd known her for two hours and I knew I'd probably never see her again after that evening – she'd said as much – and just at that moment – just for that moment – I felt that I was truly, passionately loved. I felt surrounded by it – as if the air itself was perfumed with love, drunk with love – do you know what I'm saying? I knew that this was just a moment, that it wouldn't last. As I felt her breath warm on my hand I was already living the experience in my memory. It was already over. She was one of those who had been trampled underfoot. It was an episode – that very word occurred to me at the time. I felt eternal – and I knew that this would be one of the defining moments in the girl's life – I knew it for certain. One often feels, 'Tomorrow this will all be over,' but this was different. For the girl who lay at my feet, I was the whole world. The love she surrounded me with was holy and endless. One recognises these things. I believe that. At that moment she thought of nothing but me, and for me, she was already in the past, ephemeral, an episode…

Different translations are published as single editions by Methuen and Absolute Classics (Oberon Books).

MR PAUL PRY (1826)
by glas William Jerrold

glas William Jerrold (1803–1857) was house dramatist for the Coburg Theatre where this three act 'comic sketch' was first performed. It is a free re-working of the previous season's *Paul Pry* by John Poole. Jerrold wrote several other successful plays, including *Black-Eyed Susan* before he gave up play writing for the more lucrative world of journalism.

> *PAUL PRY is an exceptionally nosy young man, always poking his nose into other peoples' business. The play is set in an Inn in Dover. A servant is about to deliver a letter for MR OLDBUTTON, which PRY will acquire.*

PAUL: Well, I'll never do another good-natured thing again. Umph, these people are no great matters. Eh, who's this?

Got a letter?

For Oldbutton? Ah, I'm just going to him. I'll deliver it, depend on me. (*Examining the letter.*) Umph, I don't know the seal; it can't be anybody belonging to the town – eh! and yet there's a similitude to Mrs Yellowcap's hand; that woman is after all the men. She's a very curious woman – will see everything. I know she went to see the Living Skeleton when he was here, unknown to Mr Y. She went in company with Mr Camphor the doctor, in order to have the benefit of his remarks on the exhibition. Ah, I know all these things. How unhappy I could make half the husbands in this town, if I liked, but it's no business of mine. It certainly is Mrs Yellowcap's hand; I am most assured of it. 'Oldbutton' – there's her 'Old', I'm convinced, and I could swear to her 'button'. I'll venture a peep just to satisfy myself.

Eh! It's from Sir Spangle Rainbow, the gentleman I met here; what does he say? 'My dear sir, I should have stayed at your Inn, but a most inquisitive young puppy so annoyed me – ' Now, who can he mean? – 'so annoyed me that I was compelled to move to the George. I will, however, wait upon you in a few minutes'. Now, who can he mean? An inquisitive puppy! I shouldn't wonder if it was that Henry Dixon, he's in everybody's business, and yet I didn't see him. Eh, how shall I get into his room?

(*Going to his door.*) I'll see what he's doing. Eh! Why, he's stuffed paper into the keyhole. Now there's something very mysterious in that!

Available in *English Plays of the Nineteenth Century, Volume 4*, Ed: M R Booth, Oxford.

THE PIGEON (1912)

by John Galsworthy

See note on Galsworthy on page 9.

FERRAND is an emaciated young Frenchman, down on his luck, talking to CHRISTOPHER WELLWYN, an artist who has previously helped him.

FERRAND: Monsieur, when I was on the road this time I fell ill of a fever. It seemed to me in my illness that I saw the truth – how I was wasting in this world – I would never be good for anyone – nor anyone for me – all would go by, and I never be of it – fame, and fortune, and peace, even the necessities of life, ever mocking me. And I saw, Monsieur, so plain, that I should be vagabond all my days, and my days short, I dying in the end the death of a dog. I saw it all in my fever – clear as that flame – there was nothing for us other but the herb of death. And so, Monsieur, I wished to die. I told no-one of my fever. I lay out on the ground – it was very cold. But they would not let me die on the streets of their parishes – they took me to an Institution. Monsieur, I looked in their eyes while I lay there, and I saw more clear than the blue heaven that they thought it best I should die, although they would not let me. Then, Monsieur, naturally my spirit rose and I said, 'So much the worse for you. I will live a little more.' One is made like that. Life is sweet, Monsieur.

That little girl you had here, Monsieur – in her, too, there is something of wild-savage. She must have the joy of life. I have seen her since I came back. She has embraced the joy of life. It is not quite the same thing.

She is lost, Monsieur, as a stone that sinks in water. I can see, if she cannot. Oh! I am not to blame for that, Monsieur. It had begun well before I knew her. I do my best for her, Monsieur, but look at me! Besides, I am not good for her – it is not good for simple souls to be with those who see things clear. For the great part of mankind, to see anything is fatal.

Available in *The Plays of John Galsworthy*, Duckworth.

HOW TO SETTLE ACCOUNTS WITH YOUR LAUNDRESS (1847)
by Joseph Stirling Coyne

Joseph Stirling Coyne (1803–1868) was a successful journalist and the successful author of a number of one-act farces. He produced thirty-five of these largely forgotten pieces between 1835 and 1869, many of them performed at the Adelphi Theatre. During the same period he turned out a similar number of burlesques, extravaganzas and melodramas.

> *WHITTINGTON WIDGETTS is a West End tailor, recently come up in the world. He is planning an assignation with a lady of dubious virtue and in this, his first speech in the play, is talking first to the audience and then his servant, TWILL.*

WIDGETTS: This night I devote to the tender union of love and lobsters. The adorable Ma'amselle Cherie Bounce, the ballet dancer, at last consents to partake a little quiet supper with me here this evening. I must read her charming note once more.

'Ma'amselle Cheri Bounce presents compliments to Mr Whittington Widgetts, will feel happy to sup with Mr W.W. this evening. Ma'amselle C.B. fears that female notions don't correspond with supping with a single gent., but lobsters is stronger than prudence, therefore trusts to indulgence; at nine o'clock precise. P.S. I'll come in my blue *visite* and my native innocence and hopes you'll treat 'em with proper delicacy.'

Glorious! Angelic creature.

Kisses the letter and puts it in his waistcoat pocket.

Oh Widgetts, you lucky rascal, to have the happiness of a private and confidential supper with that magnificent girl, whose image has never left my mind since the evening I danced with her at the Casino. Twill! Twill!

TWILL enters.

You must run directly to the tavern over the way and order them to send a roast fowl and lobster in the shell, here at nine o'clock. I expect a particular party to dine with me. No, I shan't want a cigar – the party is a lady and don't smoke. The party I expect is Ma'amselle Cheri Bounce, a splendid creature, who dances on a limited income, with the strictest regard to propriety, at the Opera House and gives lessons to private pupils in the polka and waltz. I must make myself attractive for the interesting occasion. Give me the coat that has just been finished for Sir Chippin Porrage, and the waistcoat that's to be sent home tomorrow for the Honourable Cecil Harrowgate's wedding. I'll give them an air of gentility by wearing 'em this evening.

Available in *English Plays of the Nineteenth Century, Volume 4*, Ed: M R Booth, Oxford.

WOYZECK (1837)

by Georg Büchner
translated by Veronica George

See note on Büchner on page 23.

WOYZECK is a barber in a small town. Here, the military CAPTAIN is talking to him while being given a shave. This scene opens the play.

CAPTAIN: Slow down, Woyzeck. It's one thing after another with you – you're making me dizzy. Alright, you might finish ten minutes early but what good is that to me? Think about it, Woyzeck. You've got at least thirty years ahead of you – thirty whole years. Three hundred and sixty months. How many days is that? – hours? – minutes? What are you going to do with all that time? Relax, Woyzeck. Take your time.

I start worrying, you know, when I think about eternity – when I think about the world. It's food for thought, Woyzeck, you have to admit. Eternity is…eternity…and that's, well, it's eternity. If you like. On the other hand, eternity isn't eternity, it's just the twinkling of an eye. Do you see? Woyzeck, it upsets me when I think it takes a whole day for the world to rotate on its axis. What a waste of a whole day. And where's it going to end? Every time I see a millwheel going round I get depressed.

Woyzeck, why do you always look so agitated? A normal person doesn't look like that – I mean, a chap with nothing on his conscience. Say something, Woyzeck. Anything will do. What's the weather like? Windy? Don't you hate it when it's windy? I do. It really gets to me. (*Slyly.*)

I think it's a north-southerly.

(*Bursting out laughing.*) You're not listening, are you? I said, 'I think it's a north-southerly'. You're either not listening or you're incredibly stupid. You're a good enough chap in your way, I suppose, but you've got no sense of decency. Do you know what decency means, Woyzeck? It's when someone acts decently. It's a good word, but you don't understand it, do you? You've got a child out of wedlock – without benefit of clergy, as the vicar puts it. I like that phrase. 'Without benefit of clergy.' It has a certain ring to it, doesn't it?

Your trouble is that you've got no self-control. You are indecent. You can say you're only flesh and blood but, damn it, Woyzeck, when I'm lying by my window and I see a pretty pair of legs go past in white stockings, I feel love. I'm flesh and blood too, don't you see? That's where self-control comes in. The things I could waste my time on, if I wanted. But no, I'm decent.

A different translation is available in *The Plays of Georg Büchner*, Oxford.

THE LADY OF THE CAMELLIAS (1852)

by Alexandre Dumas fils
translated by Mary Patrick

Alexandre Dumas the younger (1824–95) wrote several successful (and sometimes, at the time, scandalous) plays including *The Demi-Monde, Francillon* and *Denise*. He was the son of the famous novelist of the same name whose works include *The Three Musketeers* and *The Count of Monte Cristo*. *La Dame aux Camélias*, his most famous work, began life as a novel and was to provide the inspiration for Verdi's opera, *La Traviata*.

> *MARGUERITE GAUTIER, formerly a successful courtesan, gave up her life among the demi-monde for love of ARMAND DUVAL. However, his father persuaded her to leave him, to prevent the scandal affecting the rest of the Duval family. MARGUERITE is now poverty-stricken and dying of tuberculosis. Her old friend, GASTON, has been sitting by her sick-bed all night. NANINE is MARGUERITE's maid.*

GASTON: I was born to be a nurse. Nanine is asleep. When I came at eleven last night to find out how you were, the poor girl was ready to drop with exhaustion. I, as usual, was wide awake. You had fallen asleep so I bundled Nanine off to bed, settled myself on your sofa next to that excellent fire, and have passed a beautiful night. You slept so quietly that it did me more good than if I had slept in the most luxurious bed in Paris. How are you feeling this morning?

Don't scold me. I spend enough nights on the tiles. It's much better for me to pass some of them beside a sick-bed. Besides, I have something to say to you. You are in need of money, Marguerite. When I arrived last night, there was a bailiff in the drawing-room. I paid him off and threw him out. Sssh, now. You need some ready cash, too – and I happen to have some with me – not much, I fear, for I lost damnably at cards last night and bought an obscene number of perfectly useless presents for New Year's Day. May you be well and happy all year. But, in short, here are twenty-five louis. I'm going to put them in the drawer of that little table – and when you need more, there will be more.

Now, what shall we do today? You have slept for a good eight hours and I think you should sleep some more. Between one and three the sun will be quite warm; I'll come and take you out. Wrap up warm and we'll go for a drive in a carriage – and you'll sleep well tonight, I can promise you. In the meantime, I must go and see my mother. Lord knows what she'll say to me – I haven't been near her for a fortnight. I'll have lunch with her and be here at one. What do you say?

There are several editions of *The Lady of the Camellias*, some under the well-known English title of *Camille*. One is included in *Mirrors for Man: 26 Plays of the World Drama*, Ed: Leonard Ashley, Winthrop Publishers.

THE MOLLUSC (1907)

by Hubert Henry Davies

Hubert Henry Davies (1869–1917) was educated at Manchester Grammar School and worked in the textile industry until he went to America in 1893. There he became a successful playwright and returned to Britain to continue his career with such comedies as *Mrs Gorringe's Necklace* (1901), *A Single Man* (1910) and *Doormats* (1912).

TOM KEMP is a genial, high-spirited man, brother of MRS BAXTER, who always seems to be ill. Here, he explains his theory to her husband.

TOM: Why should Dulcie be waited on hand and foot? Ill? She's as strong as a horse, always was. She's a mollusc.

A mollusc. Mollusca, subdivision of the animal kingdom. I suppose the scientific explanation is that a mollusc once married a mammal and their descendants are the human mollusc. People who are like a mollusc of the sea, which clings to a rock and lets the tide flow over its head. People who spend all their energy and ingenuity to sticking instead of moving, in whom the instinct for what I call molluscry is as dominating as an inborn vice. And it is so catching. Why, one mollusc will infect a whole household. We all had it at home. Mother was quite a famous mollusc in her time. She was bedridden for fifteen years and then, don't you remember, got up to Dulcie's wedding, to the amazement of everybody, and tripped down the aisle as lively as a kitten, and then went to bed again until she heard of something else she wanted to go to – a garden party or something. Father, he was a mollusc, too; he called it being a conservative;

he might just as well have stayed in bed, too. Ada, Charlie, Emmeline, all of them were more or less mollusky, but Dulcibella was the queen. You won't often see such a fine healthy specimen of a mollusc as Dulcie.

I'm a born mollusc. Yes, I'm energetic now, but only artificially energetic. I have to be on to myself all the time; make myself do things. That's why I chose the vigorous West and wandered from camp to camp. I made a pile in Leadville. I gambled it all away. I made another in Cripple Creek. I gave it away to the poor. If I made another, I should chuck it away. Don't you see why? Give me a competence, nothing to work for, nothing to worry about from day to day – why, I should become as famous a mollusc as dear old Mother was. It's not the same as laziness. The lazy flow with the tide. The mollusc uses force to resist pressure. It's amazing the amount of force a mollusc will use to do nothing, when it would be so much easier to do something. It's no fool, you know, it's often the most artful creature, it wriggles and squirms and even fights from the instinct not to advance. There are wonderful things about molluscry, things to make you shout with laughter, but it's sad enough, too – it can ruin the life so, not only the life of the mollusc but all the lives in the house where it dwells. Now, as to Dulcie – try telling her not to mollusc so much. Be firm with her. Next time she tells you to do a thing, tell her to do it herself.

Available in *Late Victorian Plays*, Ed: George Rowell, The World's Classics.

BRAND (1866)
by Henrik Ibsen
translated by Simon Parker

Henrik Ibsen (1828–1906) is, with Chekhov, widely regarded as one of the fathers of modern drama. *Brand* is an early play in verse, written shortly before *Peer Gynt* (1867) and was, like that play, written to be read rather than performed. Ibsen went on to write such plays as *A Doll's House* (1879), *An Enemy of the People* (1882), *Ghosts* (1882) and *Hedda Gabler* (1890).

BRAND is a discontented priest. Here, in the mountains, he has left behind his GUIDE and travelled up a dangerous pass. He looks back at the figures of the GUIDE and his SON outlined against the snow below.

BRAND

Look at the coward, groping his way home.
If you had wanted hard enough,
And only bted your strength,
I would have helped you. Weary as I am,
I could have lifted you on my weary back
And I'd have done it gladly.
Ha! Men love living. They'll sacrifice
Anything but life, anything else –
But no, life must be saved.
When I was a child, I remember
Two thoughts which made me laugh and wouldn't
                                        leave me.
An owl scared of the dark, and a fish frightened
                                        of water.

What made me think of them? Ah, well,
Because I felt the difference – sensed it, dimly –
Between what is and what ought to be;
Between having to endure and finding one's burden
Unendurable. All men are like those owls and fish,
Created to struggle in darkness,
Living in the bottom of the pond. All men
Struggle towards the shore, terrified,
Gazing up at the blank, closed eye of heaven,
                                        screaming,
'Let me have light and air…'
What was that? Could it be singing?
Yes, I could swear it is – laughter and singing.
The mist is lifting. I can see the sun,
And the mountain plain, spreading below me.
There is a crowd of happy people on the mountain
                                        top.
Two people are leaving the crowd, heading west,
Saying farewell. Light shines about them.
It almost seems as if they melt the mist in front of
                                        them,
Running hand in hand across a carpet of heather.
Perhaps they are brother and sister.
They are coming towards me.

There are many translations of Ibsen's plays, including
Michael Meyer's famous translation available from Methuen.

THE LIARS (1897)
by Henry Arthur Jones

Henry Arthur Jones (1851–1929) was a draper's assistant and commercial traveller until the success of his play, *The Silver King* (1882). He wrote a number of comedies and dramas and is perhaps best remembered for *Mrs Dane's Defence* (1900). Other titles include *Saints and Sinners* (1884), *Michael and His Lost Angel* (1896), *Whitewashing Julia* (1903) and *The Lie* (1914).

> *COLONEL SIR CHRISTOPHER DEERING is described as 'a genial handsome Englishman of about thirty-eight'. Here he is speaking to EDWARD 'NED' FALKNER, who is planning to run away with LADY JESSICA NEPEAN.*

SIR CHRISTOPHER: One moment, Ned! Now, I've nothing to say in the abstract against running away with another man's wife! There may be planets where it is not only the highest ideal morality, but where it has the further advantage of being a practical way of carrying on society. But it has one fatal defect in our country today – it won't work! You know what we English are, Ned. We're not a bit better than our neighbours but, thank God! We do pretend we are, and we do make it hot for anybody who disturbs that holy pretence. And take my word for it, my dear Lady Jessica, my dear Ned, it won't work. It's not an original experiment you're making. It has been tried before. Have you ever known it to be successful? Lady Jessica, think of the brave pioneers who have gone before you in this enterprise. They've all perished, and their bones whiten the anti-

matrimonial shore. Think of them! Charlie Gray and
Lady Rideout – flitting shabbily about the continent at
cheap *table d'hôtes* and gambling clubs, rubbing shoulders
with all the blackguards and *demi-mondaines* of Europe.
Poor old Fitz and his beauty – moping down at Farnhurst,
cut by the county, with no single occupation except to
nag and rag each other to pieces from morning to evening.
Billy Dover and Polly Atchieson cut in for fresh partners
in three weeks. George Nuneham and Mrs Sandys –
George is conducting a tram-car in New York and Mrs
Sandys – a delicate, sweet little creature, I've met her
at your receptions – she drank herself to death and died
in a hospital. Not encouraging, is it? Marriage may be
disagreeable, it may be unprofitable, it may be ridiculous;
but it isn't as bad as that! And do you think the experiment
is going to be successful in your case? Not a bit of it! –
No, Ned, hear me out! – First of all there will be the
shabby   scandal   and   the   dirty   business
of the divorce court. You won't like that. It isn't nice.
After the divorce court, what is Ned to do with you?
Take you to Africa? I do implore you, if you hope for
any happiness in that state to which it is pleasing Falkner
and Providence to call you, don't go out to Africa with
him. You'd never stand the climate and the hardships
and you'd bore each other to death in a week. Take
any of the other alternatives and find yourself stranded
in some shady hole or corner, with the solitary hope and
ambition of somehow wriggling back into respectability.
Have done with this folly. Do believe me, my dear Ned,
my dear Lady Jessica, before it is too late, do believe
me, it won't work, it won't work, it won't work!

Available in *Late Victorian Plays,* Ed: George Rowell,
The World's Classics.

SUMMERFOLK (1904)

by Maxim Gorky
translated by Simon Parker

Maxim Gorky (1868–1936) was born into poverty and wandered Russia for many years before becoming a national celebrity at the age of thirty. He is remembered for his short stories and his involvement with radical politics in the lead-up to the 1917 Russian Revolution. His plays include *The Lower Depths* (1902), *The Children of the Sun* (1905) and *Enemies* (1908).

SHALIMOV is a forty-year-old writer, discontented with the world and his place in it.

SHALIMOV: Perhaps the one thing I could do that would be absolutely sincere is to give up writing and grow cabbages, like Diocletian. But one has to eat – so I keep on writing. I don't know for whose benefit. One ought to have a clear idea of whom one is writing for – the ideal Shalimov reader. Five years ago, I knew exactly who he was and what he wanted. And then – bam! – I lost him. Quite suddenly. Lost him. That's the problem. Everywhere I go, people are saying there's a new kind of reader these days – and I have no idea who he is. I'm not talking about educated people, intellectuals, the type who'll read anything, I mean this elusive new reader. I don't understand, I really don't. But I sense it's true. I walk down the street and see people passing – certain people – and there's something quite special in their faces, something different – in their eyes. I look into those eyes and think, 'You're not going to want what I'm giving you, are you?' I gave a reading last winter, and there they were, all these eyes, gazing at me, interested, attentive, full of curiosity…and every one of those faces was alien to me. These new people don't like me, don't like my work. I'm irrelevant to them, as irrelevant as Latin. As far as they're concerned, I'm old. My ideas are old. I don't understand. Who are they? What do they like? What do they want?

A different translation is available in *Gorky: Five Plays*, Methuen.

SALOME (1892)

by Oscar Wilde

See note on Wilde on page 21. Wilde originally wrote this play in French, for Sarah Bernhardt. The translation was undertaken by his lover, Lord Alfred Douglas, and Wilde was far from happy with it.

HEROD, Tetrarch of Galilee, has become besotted with his teenage stepdaughter, SALOME, and here promises her anything her heart desires if only she will dance for him.

HEROD: Salomé, Salomé, dance for me. I pray thee dance for me. I am sad tonight. Yes, I am passing sad tonight. When I came hither I slipped in blood, which is an evil omen; and I heard, I am sure I heard in the air a beating of wings, a beating of giant wings. I cannot tell what they mean...I am sad tonight. Therefore dance for me. Dance for me, Salomé, I beseech you. If you dance for me you may ask of me what you will, and I will give it to you, even unto the half of my kingdom. I swear it, Salomé. I have sworn, Salomé. Even to the half of my kingdom. Thou wilt be passing fair as a queen, Salomé, if it please thee to ask for half of my kingdom. Will she not be fair as a queen? Ah! it is cold here! There is an icy wind, and I hear...wherefore do I hear in the air this beating of wings? Ah! One might fancy a bird, a huge black bird that hovers over the terrace. Why can I not see it, this bird? The beat of its wings is terrible. The breath of the wind on its wings is terrible. It is a chill wind. Nay, but it is not cold, it is hot. I am choking. Pour water on my hands. Give me snow to eat. Loosen my mantle. Quick, quick! Loosen my mantle. Nay, but leave it. It is my garland that hurts me, my garland of roses. The flowers are like fire. They have burned my forehead.

He tears the wreath from his head and throws it onto the table.

Ah! I can breathe now. How red those petals are! They are like stains of blood on the cloth. That does not matter. You must not find symbols in everything you see. It makes life impossible. It were better to say that stains of blood are as lovely as rose petals. It were far better to say that... But we will not speak of this. Now I am happy, I am passing happy. Have I not the right to be happy? Your daughter is going to dance for me. Will you not dance for me, Salomé? You have promised to dance for me.

Available in *The Complete Works of Oscar Wilde*, Collins.

CHILDREN OF THE SUN (1905)

by Maxim Gorky
translated by Simon Parker

See note on Gorky on page 48.

PROTASSOV is a middle-aged student of Natural Science. He is talking to his wife, ELYENA.

PROTASSOV: Elyena, I must tell you something. You see, something very silly has happened. Has Melanya Borisovna gone? Oh good. Now, don't laugh, but... Oh Lord... She seems to have fallen in love with me. Just...well, just fallen in love. What do you think of that? Of course, I've never given her the slightest encouragement. Stop laughing! This is serious. Oh, do stop laughing, it's awful, really awful. Here she was, a minute ago, on her knees, kissing my trousers...and my hand...this hand!

(*Cross.*) Well, Elyena, I'm very surprised you should react like this. I promise you she wasn't joking. She offered to give me all her money... She said, 'I want to live with you, my darling Pavel.' Yes, she called me 'darling' and 'Pavel'. You do believe that I haven't encouraged her, don't you? She has a funny smell, you know, like saltpetre. Why are you laughing?

(*Offended.*) It isn't funny at all. I was completely taken aback. It's all extremely silly. Oh, I managed to say something to her, some nonsense, but my head was spinning. And then, I swear, she was completely serious. And she told me that you knew all about it – and I couldn't work out what she meant, what it was you were supposed to know all about – and then I didn't know whether or not to tell you because...well, you might be very cross with me, and it really wasn't my fault...

You did know? Why on earth didn't you warn me? But if you knew... Oh, well I suppose that's alright, isn't it. Shall we have some tea? And will you sort it out for me?

A different translation is available in *Gorky: Five Plays*, Methuen.

THE SECOND MRS TANQUERAY (1893)
by Sir Arthur Wing Pinero

Sir Arthur Wing Pinero (1854–1934) was born in Islington of Portuguese extraction. He began his career as a lawyer but became an actor at the age of twenty. He acted with many of the great Victorian 'names', including Squire Bancroft and Sir Henry Irving. From the age of twenty-eight he concentrated on writing and was knighted in 1909. He is best remembered for his comedies, *The Magistrate* (1885), *The Schoolmistress* (1896), *Dandy Dick* (1897) and *Trelawney of the 'Wells'* (1898). However, Pinero wrote a number of serious plays dealing with social issues of the day and influenced by Ibsen. This is one of his serious dramas.

> *CAYLEY DRUMMLE is described by the author as 'a neat little man of about five and forty, in manner bright, airy and debonair, but with an undercurrent of seriousness'.*

> *He is a close friend of AUBREY TANQUERAY, who has just announced his intention of marrying again. He is speaking to other guests at TANQUERAY's house.*

DRUMMLE: Deuce take it, the man's second marriage mustn't be another mistake! He married a Miss Herriott; that was in the year eighteen – confound dates! – twenty years ago. She was a lovely creature – by Jove, she was; by religion a Roman Catholic. She was one of your cold sort, you know – all marble arms and black velvet. I remember her with painful distinctness as the only woman who ever made me nervous! He loved her – to distraction, as they say. Jupiter, how fervently that poor fellow courted her! But I don't believe she even allowed him to squeeze her fingers. She *was* an iceberg! As for kissing, the mere contact would have given him chapped lips. However, he married her and took her away, the latter greatly to my relief. Abroad. I imagine he gratified her by renting a villa in Lapland, but I don't know. After a while, they returned, and then I saw how woefully Aubrey had miscalculated results. He had reckoned, poor wretch, that in the early days of marriage she would thaw. But she didn't. I used to picture him closing his doors and making up the fire in the hope of seeing her features relax. Bless her, the thaw never set in! I believe she kept a thermometer in her stays and always registered ten degrees below zero. However, in time, a child came – a daughter.

It made matters worse. Frightened at her failure to stir up in him some sympathetic religious belief, she determined upon strong measures with regard to the child. He opposed her for a miserable year or so, but she wore him down, and the insensible little brat was placed in a convent, first in France, then in Ireland. Not long afterwards the mother died – strangely enough of fever – the only warmth, I believe, that ever came to that woman's body. The child is living – if you call it living. Miss Tanqueray – a young woman of nineteen now – is at the Loretto convent at Armagh. She professes to have found her true vocation in a religious life and in a month or two will take her final vows. You remember his visit to Ireland last month? That was to wish his girl goodbye. I think he must have had a lingering hope that the girl would relent.

Available in *Pinero: Three Plays*, Methuen.

HIS HOUSE IN ORDER (1906)
by Sir Arthur Wing Pinero

See note on Pinero on page 54.

*HILARY JESSON is a genial, fresh cosmopolitan man
in his thirties, British Commissioner of the island of
Santa Guardia. Here he stands up to his MP brother,
FILMER, about the way FILMER's young wife, NINA,
has been treated. The RIDGELEYS, whom he
mentions, are the aristocratic parents of FILMER's
deceased first wife.*

HILARY: I bring a distinct charge. I charge these people
with malice. I charge them – as she, herself, has already
charged them – with a jealous hatred of the girl you
have married. I charge them with pursuing – deliberately
pursuing – a system of pitiless persecution of Nina.
I mean the Ridgeleys, of course. Oh, I don't care a rap
whether or not they are self-deceivers, whether or not
theirs is an unconscious hypocrisy. Because they hug
themselves with a belief in their own righteousness, they
are the more pernicious. I'd wipe out the whole class
to which these Ridgeleys belong, Filmer – exterminate
it ruthlessly. It's a class that brings everything that's
good in the world – virtue and charity, and religion –
into odium and contempt. Its members, individually and
collectively, are the pests of humanity. And I charge
you with abetting the Ridgeleys – tacitly abetting them
– in their treatment of this girl. I charge you with
harbouring people in your home – which is hers – who
you *know* despise her, and who are constantly wounding
and humiliating her. Yes, you know it; and wince under

it; and occasionally, in a half-hearted fashion, try to shield her. So you've not even the excuse of ignorance. And what's your justification? You find her wanting. You find her wanting in qualities you've no right to demand of her; qualities, in some minds, less admirable than those she's endowed with. Therefore you break your bargain with her – the bargain every man enters into when he marries; and you *cheat* her – cheat her of the protection and comfort which are her due. You find her wanting? Well, I find *you* wanting. I find you wanting in dignity, and manliness and independence. And I raise my voice against what I see going on here; I protest against it with all the strength that's in me; I protest against it; oppose it; forbid it.

He brings his fist down heavily upon the table.

Forgive me.

Available in a single edition from Heinemann.

THE ADMIRABLE CRICHTON (1902)
by J M Barrie

Sir James Matthew Barrie (1860–1937), most famous as the author of *Peter Pan* (1904) began his career as a journalist before writing for the theatre. His plays include *Quality Street* (1901), *What Every Woman Knows* (1908), *The Twelve Pound Look* (1910) and *Dear Brutus* (1917). He also wrote a number of prose works, the most famous of which is *The Little Minister* (1891).

CRICHTON is the butler of LORD LOAM. When the family are shipwrecked on a desert island, the old social order becomes irrelevant and CRICHTON becomes effective leader of the group. Here he is speaking to LADY MARY LASENBY, LORD LOAM's attractive daughter, who has become enamoured of CRICHTON's manly behaviour.

CRICHTON: I have always tried to do the right thing on this island. Above all, Polly, I want to do the right thing by you. I want a greater reward than your trust. (*Taking her hand.*) Am I playing the game? Bill Crichton would always like to play the game. If we were in England –

I am thinking, Polly, of two people whom neither of us has seen for a long time – Lady Mary Lasenby and one Crichton, a butler. I had nigh forgotten them. He has had a chance, that butler – he's had a chance in these years of becoming a man, and he has tried to take it. There have been many failures, but there has been some success, and with it all I have let the past drop away, and turned my back on it. There's something so grand to me in feeling myself a man. That butler seems a far-away figure to me now, and not myself – I hail him, but we scarce know each other – if I am to bring him back it can only be done by force – for in my soul he is now abhorrent to me. But if I thought it best for you – if I thought it best for you, I'd drag him back – I swear as an honest man I would bring him back to you with all his obsequious ways and deferential airs and let you see who the man you call your Gov. melt for ever into him who was your servant.

I say these like a king, you say. I sometimes feel – I say it harshly, it is hard to say, and all the time there is another voice within me crying – it is the voice of Nature. Polly, some people hold that the soul but leaves one human tenement for another, and so lives on through the ages. In some past existence I may have been a king – who knows? It has come to me so naturally, not as if I had had to work it out but as if I remembered. I am lord over all – they are but hewers of wood and drawers of water for me – these shores are mine – why should I hesitate? I have no longer any doubt. I do believe I *am* doing the right thing. Polly, dear Polly. Dear Polly, I have grown to love you. Will you let John Treherne make us man and wife?

Available in *J M Barrie, Plays and Stories*, Everyman.

QUALITY STREET (1901)
by J M Barrie

See note on Barrie on page 58.

Ten years previously, VALENTINE was a young man gently courting PHOEBE, before he joined the army to fight in the Napoleonic wars. Now PHOEBE makes her living running a small school and has lost her looks and vivacity. All is not lost, however. When VALENTINE comes back into her life, she pretends to be LIVVY, her own niece, and sets out to win VALENTINE's heart. Here, VALENTINE has just returned from a ball with 'MISS LIVVY' and reveals his true feelings.

VALENTINE: It was at the balls that I fell in love with Miss Phoebe – she who was never at a ball. But I must not tell you – it might hurt you.

Then on your head be the blame. It is you who have made me love her, Miss Livvy. It is odd and yet very simple. You who so resembled her as she was, for an hour, ma'am, you bewitched me – yes, I confess it – but 'twas only for an hour. How like, I cried at first but soon it was, How unlike! There was almost nothing she would have said that you said; you did so much that she would have scorned to do. Miss Phoebe's lady-likeness on which she set such store, that I used to make merry of the word – I gradually perceived that it is a woman's most beautiful adornment, and the casket which contains all the adorable qualities that go to the making of a perfect female. When Miss Livvy rolled her eyes – oh – oh! It made me the more complacent that never in her life had Miss Phoebe been guilty of the slightest deviation from the strictest propriety. I was always conceiving her in your place – oh, it was monstrous unfair to you – I stood looking at you, Miss Livvy, and seeing in my mind *her*, and all the pretty things she did, and you did not do; why, ma'am, that is how I fell in love with Miss Phoebe at the balls. Ma'am, tell me, do you think there is any hope for me?

I shall go to her. 'Miss Phoebe,' I will say – oh, ma'am, so reverently – 'Miss Phoebe, my beautiful, most estimable of women, let me take care of you for evermore.' Ah! You may laugh at a rough soldier so enamoured, but 'tis true. 'Marry me, Miss Phoebe,' I shall say, 'and I will take you back through those years of hardships that have made your sweet eyes so patient. Instead of growing older you shall grow younger. We will travel back together to pick up the many little joys and pleasures you had to pass by when you trod that thorny path alone'.

Nay, Miss Phoebe has loved me. You have said it. She will be my wife yet.

Published in a single edition by Samuel French.

MONEY (1840)

by Edward Bulwer-Lytton

See note on Bulwer-Lytton and *Money* on page 18.

GRAVES is a solicitor of middle-years, recently bereaved, and here displays his 'grave' temperament.

GRAVES: Everything in life is sad. Be comforted, Miss Vesey. True, you have lost an uncle, but I – I have lost a wife! – such a wife! the first of her sex and the second cousin of the defunct. Nothing in life can charm me now.

(*Aside.*) A monstrous fine woman, that!

It is an atrocious world. But the astronomers say that there is a travelling comet which must set it on fire some day, and that's a comfort. Ah, yes – read the newspapers. They'll tell you what this world is made of. Daily calendars of roguery and woe! Here, advertisements from quacks, money-lenders, cheap warehouses and spotted boys with two heads. So much for dupes and imposters! Turn to the other column – police reports, bankruptcies, swindling, forgeries, and a biographical sketch of the snub-nosed man who murdered his three little cherubs at Pentonville. Do you fancy these but exceptions to the general virtue and health of the nation? Turn to the leading article and your hair will stand on end at the horrible wickedness or melancholy idiotism of that half the population who think differently from yourself. In my day I have seen already some eighteen crises, six annihilations of Agriculture and Commerce, four overthrows of the Church, and three last, final, awful and irremediable destructions of the entire Constitution! And there's a newspaper!

No, I never laugh. I haven't laughed since the death of my sainted Maria. I don't laugh because... What? Because I have lost my front teeth? Upon my word! Ha, ha, ha. That's too good. Capital. Ha, ha, ha.

Available in *English Plays of the Nineteenth Century, Volume 3*, Ed: M R Booth, Oxford.

HER SOUL (1898)

by Amelia Rosselli
translated by Veronica George

Amelia Rosselli (1870–1954) was born in Venice and settled in Rome. *Her Soul* was her first play and was written as a riposte to Giuseppe Giacosa's *The Rights of the Soul*. Rosselli wrote several other plays, both in Italian and in the Venetian dialect, including *Illusion* (1901), *The Fixed Idea* (1906), *Father's Partner* (1909) and *Emma the Lioness* (1924), about the life of Lady Hamilton. She also wrote short stories and books for children.

> *SILVIO, a lawyer, has been involved with OLGA DE VELARIS, a painter. Now married to GRAZIANA MAURI, he looks back at his past relationship with OLGA.*

SILVIO: Olga, how truly you spoke when you said 'I was more yours than if we had been lovers.' Do you remember? It is a dear memory which keeps me alive when I am alone and makes me feel better. The memory of it makes me live for you, just as I did when we shared our love. Is that so much to ask for? Do you really think Graziana would be offended if she could see inside my soul? Don't you think that, by now, I've earned the right to my own soul? Since I married her, I have never felt – not even for a minute – that Graziana's soul was mine. You only have to look at her... Yet I fought so hard to win her. After I made that terrible error, I told myself that it would be wrong to make her a victim of my mistake. I tried to find a way of rebuilding my shattered life. I tried diligently and honestly. I thought that, if she helped me, I might be able to do it. I tried to rouse her interest in my work. I asked her advice, I shared my projects with her, I talked about the future. I tried so hard to establish that bond between us, that connection of feeling and thought, the bond without which there can be no possession. But she didn't understand me. She would interrupt me to read the poem the Marquis had written in her album or play me the song that someone had composed for her. I wanted her to see me as her husband, the one who shared her life – but all she saw in me was the one who could give her her freedom, that freedom she longed for so much. Little by little, a silence set in between us. Even when we spoke, that silence was still there.

Ironic, isn't it? Destiny gave me what I asked for – the masculine triumph of looking at her and saying to myself, 'No other man has caressed that body.' What a triumph! Perhaps I possessed her body but her soul was not mine, nor had it ever been. I was overcome with jealousy that perhaps her soul belonged to someone else – the worst kind of adultery,

A different translation is available in *Modern Drama by Women, 1880s–1930s*, Ed: Katherine E. Kelly, Routledge.

THE SECOND MRS TANQUERAY (1893)
by Sir Arthur Wing Pinero

See note on Pinero and *The Second Mrs Tanqueray* on page 54.

AUBREY TANQUERAY is forty-two, 'handsome, winning in manner, his speech and bearing retaining some of the qualities of young-manhood.' He has recently married PAULA, a woman with a shady past. PAULA has been quite honest about her background. The relationship starts to go wrong when ELLEAN, AUBREY's pious and cold daughter from an earlier marriage, comes to stay with them. Here he remonstrates with PAULA.

AUBREY: Now listen to me. Fond as you are, Paula, of harking back to your past, there's one chapter of it you always let alone. I've never asked you to speak of it; you've never offered to speak of it. I mean the chapter that relates to the time when you were – like Ellean.

I know what you were like at Ellean's age. You hadn't a thought that wasn't a wholesome one, you hadn't an impulse that didn't tend towards good, you never harboured a notion you couldn't have gossiped about to a parcel of children. And this was a very few years back – there are days now when you look like a schoolgirl – but think of the difference between the two Paulas. You'll have to think hard, because after a cruel life one's perceptions grow a thick skin. But, for God's sake, do think till you get these two images clearly in your mind, and then ask yourself what sort of friend such a woman as you are today would have been for the girl of seven or eight years ago.

You're blind, Paula. You're blind. You! Every belief that a young, pure-minded girl holds sacred – that you once held sacred – you now make a target for a jest, for a sneer, a paltry cynicism. I tell you, you're not mistress any longer of your thoughts or your tongue. Why, how often, sitting between you and Ellean, have I seen her cheeks turn scarlet as you've rattled off some tale that by rights belongs to the club or the smoking-room. Have you noticed the blush? If you have, has the cause of it ever struck you? And this is the girl you say you love, I admit that you *do* love, whose love you expect in return. Oh Paula, I make the best, the only excuse for you, when I say you're blind.

Available in *Pinero: Three Plays*, Methuen.

A FLORENTINE TRAGEDY
by Oscar Wilde

See note on Wilde on page 21. *A Florentine Tragedy* is an undated fragment, an early work which has never been professionally staged.

SIMONE, a merchant, has been betrayed by his wife, BIANCA, with the wealthy LORD GUIDO. In this extract he is talking to them both. Neither of them realise that he knows about their liaison.

SIMONE

Good night, my lord.
Fetch a pine torch, Bianca. The old staircase
Is full of pitfalls, and the churlish moon
Grows, like a miser, niggard of her beams,
And hides her face behind a muslin mask
As harlots do when they go forth to snare
Some wretched soul in sin. Now, I will get
Your cloak and sword. Nay, pardon, my good Lord,
It is but meet that I should wait on you,
Who have so honoured my poor burgher's house,
Drunk of my wine, and broken bread, and made
Yourself a sweet familiar. Oftentimes
My wife and I will talk of this fair night
And its great issues.

                Why, what a sword is this!
Ferrara's temper, pliant as a snake,
And deadlier, I doubt not. With such steel
One need fear nothing in the moil of life.

I never touched so delicate a blade.
I have a sword, too, somewhat rusted now.
We men of peace are taught humility,
And to bear many burdens on our backs,
And not to murmur at an unjust world,
And to endure unjust indignities.
We are taught that and, like the patient Jew,
Find profit in our pain. Yet I remember
How once upon the road to Padua
A robber sought to take my pack-horse from me.
I slit his throat and left him. I can bear
Dishonour, public insult, many shames,
Shrill scorn and open contumely, but he
Who filches from me something that is mine,
Ay! though it be the meanest trencher-plate
From which I feed my appetite – oh! he
Perils his soul and body in the theft
And dies for his small sin. From what strange clay
We men are moulded.
I wonder, my Lord Guido, if my sword
Is better tempered that this steel of yours?
Shall we make trial?

Available in *The Complete Works of Oscar Wilde*, Collins.

NEW MEN AND OLD ACRES (1869)
by Tom Taylor and
Augustus William Dubourg

Augustus William Dubourg (1830–1910) is little known, though he published *Four Original Plays* in 1883 and also collaborated with Taylor on *A Sister's Penance* (1866). Tom Taylor (1817–1880) was a prolific and popular playwright, writing nine comedies for the Haymarket between 1857 and 1869. He subsequently turned his hand to serious drama. He is remembered for *The Contested Election* (1859), *The Overland Route* (1860) and *Our American Cousin* (1861). *New Men and Old Acres* was an immediate success and frequently revived in the 1870s, one London production starring Ellen Terry.

> *BUNTER is a self-made man, extremely rich but disapproved of by his more upper-class connections because of his accent and his vulgarity. BUNTER is a shrewd businessman and has a warm heart. He is talking to his wife who has just spent a great deal of money on a family tree.*

BUNTER: One hundred and thirty pounds?! Here, I've just been robbed of two thousand, given away a lot of beautiful bricks – and you must pick my pocket of a hundred and thirty besides! You're always doing it, Maria. It's the last load of straws that breaks the camel's back. A hundred and thirty pounds for a bit of parchment and a lot of stuff and 'umbug.

The Bunters was Anglo-Saxons before the Conquest, was they? Well, I'm glad they found that out. It's pleasant to know other people had ancestors as well as them aristocrats at the Abbey. (*Taking the pedigree.*) As

I shall have to pay for it, I may as well take the benefit. Hollo! What's the meaning of them painted Dutch ovens?

(*Reading*.) 'The Bunters, an ancient Anglo-Saxon family, settled originally about Wethering Sett, County of Suffolk.' I wonder 'ow they knew that; I didn't. 'Their lands were probably confiscated by the Conqueror.' Very likely; you see, the aristocracy was down on us, Maria, even that early – 'owin' no doubt to the stubborn resistance of the Saxon landowner'. I'm glad we resisted. It was 'ighly creditable to us under the circumstances. I dare say most people of property knocked under. 'The family were not prominent under the Plantagenet.' No, I never heard we were. A poor lot them Plantagenet Bunters. 'Nor are we accurately informed which side they espoused during the Wars of the Roses.' That's a pity. Let's 'ope it was the side that came uppermost. 'At the Revolution, we find a Bunter parish constable of Wimmering.' You see, Maria, we'd come down by that time – 'and the name occurs frequently in Suffolk registers under the first three Georges, but without public function'. No, we didn't seem to care for public functions – a retiring family, the Bunters.

Oh, now there's something about me. 'The present representative of the family is Benjamin Bunter, Esquire, honourably known in connection with extensive public works and financial operations in all parts of the world.' That's very neatly put. 'He is the only son of the late eminent Nonconformist divine, the Rev Boanerges Bunter of Ball's Pond, Islington.' Ah, how proud the old man would have been, if he could have read all that, in the coal and 'tatur shed where he worked all week, afore taking the pulpit at the Sniggs Rents, Ebenezer.

No, Maria, I don't grudge the money now. Considering all the trouble they must have taken to find out all them facts about the Bunters, from the Anglo-Saxons before the Conquest down to Ball's Pond, I don't mind.

Available in *English Plays of the Nineteenth Century, Volume 3*, Ed: M R Booth, Oxford.

THE LOWER DEPTHS (1902)

by Maxim Gorky
translated by Simon Parker

See note on Gorky on page 48. *The Lower Depths*, set in a Moscow doss house, is considered his masterpiece.

LUKA, aged sixty, is a palmer. He is talking to other down and outs.

LUKA: Somebody has to be kind. People need to be pitied. After all, Christ pitied everyone and told us to pity each other. And it's good when you can take pity on someone. I once worked as a caretaker in a house outside Tomsk. It was owned by an engineer. Now, this house stood all by itself in the forest – a very lonely spot, it was. Winter in Siberia. And there was I, all alone. That was fine, I didn't mind it. Then one day – this noise. Someone trying to break in. Thieves. I picked up a gun and went out, looked around. There were two of them, trying to open a window. So busy they were, they didn't even notice me. I shouted, 'Oy! Get away from there'. They turned round. One of them came towards me with an axe. 'Stop, or I'll shoot!' I shouted. I kept training the gun on one, then the other. And you know what? They went down on their knees and begged me to let them go.

Well, I just lost my temper – it was the axe did it, I think. 'I told you to go,' I said, 'and instead you wield that thing at me. So now,' I said to one of them, 'you go over there and break a branch off that tree'. Well, he did. And I said to the other one, 'You lie down. Go on, face down!' And he did. And I said to the first one, 'Now, you whip him with that branch'. And he did. They both did as I told them, and ended up giving each other a right good whipping. And when they'd finished, they said, 'Look, grandpa, we're starving. Have you got any bread? Just a crust? We've had nothing to eat for days'. (*Laughs.*) They'd run away from a penal colony, see. Turned out to be nice lads. They ended up staying with me for the whole winter. But if I hadn't taken pity on them, maybe they'd have come back in the middle of the night and killed me or something, then they've had ended up back in the courts and back in another penal colony. And where's the good in that? Prison doesn't teach a man to be good, and nor does Siberia. Only another poor soul can do that. It's true. One soul can teach good to another soul. It's not complicated.

A different translation is available in *Gorky: Five Plays*, Methuen.

THE MAGISTRATE (1895)
by Sir Arthur Wing Pinero

See note on Pinero on page 54.

AENEAS POSKET, a respectable magistrate, has married a woman who has lied about her age. This poses no problem in itself save that it means that her nineteen-year-old son, CIS, is treated as if he were fourteen. POSKET and the boy have spent an evening out on the town, which has spiraled into mayhem. Next morning, in the magistrate's room at the Mulberry St Police Court, POSKET is discovered in a dreadful state – his evening suit muddy and rumpled, his linen soiled and crumpled, a strip of black plaster across his nose and in a state of extreme exhaustion.

POSKET: Where can that boy have got to? If I could only remember how, when and where we parted! I think it was at Kilburn. Let me think – first, the kitchen. (*Putting his hand to his side as if severely bruised.*) Oh! Cis was alright, because I fell underneath; I felt it was my duty to do so. Then what occurred? A dark room, redolent of onions and cabbages, and Cis dragging me over the stone floor, saying, 'We're in the scullery, Guv, let's try and find the tradesmen's door.' Next, the night air – oh, how refreshing! 'Cis, my boy, we'll both learn a lesson from tonight – never deceive!' Where are we? In Argyle Street. 'Look out, Guv, they're after us!' (*Rising in agitation.*) Then – then, as Cis remarked when we were getting over the railings in Portman Square – then the fun began. We over into the Square – they after us. Over again, into Baker Street. Down Baker Street, curious recollections while running of my first visit, as a happy child, to Madame Tussaud's, and wondering whether her removal had affected my fortunes. (*Sinks on knees by chair.*) 'Come on, Guv – you're getting blown.' Where are we? Park Road. What am I doing? (*Rising.*) Getting up out of a puddle. St John's Wood. The cricket ground. 'I say, Guv, what a run this would be at Lords, wouldn't it? And no fear of being run out, either, more of being run in.' 'What road is this, Cis?' Maida Vale. Good gracious! A pious aunt of mine once lived in Hamilton Terrace; she never thought I should come to this. 'Guv?' 'Yes, my boy?' 'Let's get this kind-hearted coffee-stall keeper to hide us.' We apply. 'Will you assist two unfortunate gentlemen?' 'No, blowed if I will.' 'Why not?' ''Cos I'm agoin' to join in the chase after you.' Ah! Off again, along Maida Vale. On, on, Heaven knows how or where till, at last, no sign of pursuit, no Cis, no breath, and the early Kilburn buses starting for town. (*He sinks into a chair, wipes his forehead, rising, after a pause.*) Then I came back again, and not much too soon for the Court.

He looks in the mirror of the washstand and utters a low groan.

Oh, how shockingly awful I look and how stiff and sore I feel.

He starts to wash.

What a weak, double-faced creature to be a magistrate. I really ought to get some member of Parliament to ask a question about me in the House. Where's the soap? I shall put five pounds and costs into the poor box tomorrow. But I deserve a most severe caution. (*Reflectively.*) Ah, perhaps

I shall get that from Agatha. When Wormington arrives,
I will borrow some money and send out for a black cravat. All
my money is in my overcoat at the Hotel des Princes. If the
police seize it, there is some consolation in knowing that the
money will never be returned to me.

Available in *Pinero: Three Plays*, Methuen.